Revelation *to* Restoration

Deana Elliott

ISBN 979-8-88616-311-7 (paperback)
ISBN 979-8-88616-312-4 (digital)

Christian Faith Publishing
832 Park Avenue
Meadville, PA 16335
www.christianfaithpublishing.com

Printed in the United States of America

This book is dedicated to God, my Father. Your love for me was like a lighthouse that brought me safely back to You after many years of living fractured, tormented, and in darkness. You have given me everything, and I will always do my best to joyfully surrender my life to You and walk in radical obedience.

To my greatest earthly treasures, my husband, John, and son, Jordan. I love you beyond words. I am deeply blessed that you have given me the privilege of knowing what it feels like to love and be loved in ways I never expected or thought possible.

I would also like to give a "shout-out" to my amazing church, my pastor, the entire pastoral staff, and all my church family. Thank you for providing me a safe environment where I could hear God's truth, receive revelation, encounter Jesus on a very personal level, find community, and begin my journey of healing and deliverance.

Writing this book was a complete labor of love for me, and I am thankful that out of all the books you could have purchased for yourself or someone, you chose this one. This book is full of personal revelation and revelation I have learned from others along the way. It is about revelation that will bring you restoration if you are willing to put in the work to submit yourself to the journey, which is not always easy. However, once you begin seeing small changes in yourself, it will make you want to keep pressing in and moving forward.

The revelation in this book has been a part of my own journey and still is. I continue to walk through healing and deliverance from childhood trauma, life's hurts, consequences of past choices, and generational iniquities. Healing and deliverance is not a one-time occasion. There can be many layers to healing, and just when you think you have been healed, a new situation comes along to put pressure on you and exposes you have another layer of healing to walk through. This is the way it is for everyone, and we will continue to need healing or deliverance until we walk into eternity.

As you read this book, let the Lord guide you through it. If you feel like you need to stop on a specific day and stay there for a few days or a week, then allow yourself that time. After reading this book, you may feel you need to read it again immediately or several times each year. I guarantee the Lord will reveal something new to you every time you read it, which will bring you more healing and closer to Him. Although this book is written as a book for thirty days, there are no guidelines. Just read it, reflect on the message for that day, and make the choice to walk through forgiveness or repentance and watch your faithful and loving Father transform you into the person He created you to be. I came from a place of severe darkness and depravity, so much so that I could feel darkness literally flowing through my veins. Now, I am walking in His love, light, and freedom. I give Him all the glory and honor for how He has transformed me and how He continues to heal me. What He has done for me, He can do the same for you and more.

I pray this book awakens something inside of you where you long for a deeper relationship with the Father and you cannot help but to chase after Him. I hope you realize that the restoration you can walk in and everything you can have access to from the Father is simply because you are walking in intimate relationship with Him and have allowed Jesus to be the King of your entire life. You do not have to earn it, and none of us deserve it. But because of Jesus, we have access to it all.

In this book, you will find pages for writing personal and reflection notes as you read each day. I encourage you to jot down your initial thoughts and to fill those pages with what the Lord is revealing to you. As you continue to use this book as a tool to pursue new levels of healing and deliverance, you will be able to go back and add to the revelation you have already received. You can also go back and read your notes to see how much you have grown spiritually.

There is a word used in this book I would like to give some depth to. Many people have heard the word repent before; however, I believe the church and Christians in general have thrown this word around until its meaning has been watered down. Repentance is a huge part of the life of a follower of Christ and is necessary so we may walk broken and remorseful for our sins and offenses toward God.

When we repent, we are not only sorrowful, but we are choosing to turn our faces back to God and turn away from whatever is dishonoring God. Repentance is not just an act, it is a change of the mind and heart that frees us to walk down the path of righteousness and into a deeper relationship with the Father." As a Christian, simply put, repentance must become a way of life if you want to live a holy life and have access to every good thing God has for you.

I bless you on your journey, beloved. I come into agreement with everything God has for you and pray that you will walk out God's purposes for your life.

Day 1

So then, my beloved, just as you have always obeyed,
not as in my presence only, but now much more in
my absence, work out your own salvation with fear
and trembling; for it is God who is at work in you,
both to desire and to work for His good pleasure.

—Philippians 2:12–13 (NASB)

Search me, O God, and know my heart! Try me and
know my thoughts! And see if there be any grievous
way in me, and lead me in the way everlasting!

—Psalm 139:23–24 (ESV)

It really takes a supernatural courage to walk through deliverance and healing. It takes a brave person to let Jesus have access to the things that haunt you, to the dark and cavernous places of your soul. I have never seen a more valiant person than someone who is willing to deal with their issues and fight for complete restoration without giving up.

It is not enough to sit back and wait for the Lord to let you wake up one day completely restored and free from life issues and unhealed wounds. While the Father is all about signs, wonders, and miracles, He is more about having personal encounters with someone who has an open heart, is vulnerable, and is willing to walk through the difficulty that often comes with healing and deliverance. Believe me it can be extremely messy and can be frustrating. However, it is so worth it to become who you truly are created to be.

Unfortunately, while some people do get completely delivered when they receive salvation, for most people, healing does not come that way. It comes through the encounters we have with the Father, which allow Him access to plow through all the debris, clean us up, and restore us to our rightful place as heirs to His kingdom. The Father is a gentleman and will not push Himself on you, but He has given all an open invitation to seek Him and find Him if we seek Him with all our heart (Jeremiah 29:13).

As you begin this journey toward restoration, I want you to remember something very important about the process of walking through healing. When the Lord begins to tear down the spiritual strongholds that have held you captive, godly strongholds must be built to protect you from attack.

Building godly strongholds comes through continuous intimate encounters with the Lord. They are built from a solid prayer life, praying in the Spirit, meditating on God's Word, and being able to recall His Word and declare it over your life when the enemy tries to sneak back in to try to take back territory he has lost.

Day 1 Reflection

This devotional is about going deeper. It is about having encounters with the Father, asking Him to search your heart and to find the things that do not align with His Word and what He has written over your life. It is about healing, restoration, and moving toward a pure intimate relationship with Him through revelation and reflection. Are you ready to take a dive into the deeper things of the Lord? I am excited just thinking about what He has in store for you over the next thirty days, especially as you reflect and write down what you feel the Lord is saying to you. Please remember the Holy Spirit comes to convict us so we will turn back to God. The enemy wants to condemn us to keep us separated from God.

Today, as you begin this journey, I want to pray over you.

Father, I ask You to open all the senses of the beloved person who is reading this devotion so they may encounter You in every way possible. I ask Your Holy Spirit to reveal Your presence to them so they would feel safe to be vulnerable and keep nothing from You because You know it all and yet You still love them very much. I pray as they feel Your love, it would lead them to repentance, healing, and deliverance. I pray it will begin to break off everything that does not bow its knee to the name of Jesus so it can bring them back into alignment with whom they were designed to be. I ask this in the name of Jesus. Amen.

Personal Notes

Day 2

Examine me, Lord, and put me to the test;
Refine my mind and my heart.

—Psalm 26:2 (NASB)

Agree with your adversary quickly, while you are
on the way with him, lest your adversary deliver
you to the judge, the judge hand you over to
the officer, and you be thrown into prison.

—Matthew 5:25 (NKJV)

One morning I heard the Lord tell me, "Your greatest adversary will bring your greatest deliverance." I know everything the Father has for me is good because I know He has a deep love for me as His daughter. However, I do not think any of us enjoy going through discomfort or productive pain to be refined and walk in His glory. Let me be honest and say sometimes it is exhausting and I want to give up. Yet, I know how important it is that I keep pressing on.

When I really think about it, I could almost chuckle about how ridiculous it seems that a person who is the greatest thorn in my side can be the very person who will bring about the greatest amount of deliverance and healing in my life. One thing I have realized walking through those situations is it makes me feel gratitude toward my adversary and even begins to change my heart toward them.

In the end, our enemy could become our ally, or they may continue to be our adversary. It matters not! What matters is that we allow ourselves to be refined and become one with Jesus. Imagine being a woodworking project where we start out as a piece of wood that is being sanded with the coarsest sandpaper. With each sanding, the sandpaper becomes finer, and the wood becomes easier to sand. Once the process is complete, we find what was once just a log is now something beautiful and of great value.

The question we must ask ourselves is, Are we willing to participate in the opportunity to change and grow? Are we going to willingly and wholeheartedly be obedient and submit ourselves to what God wants to do in our lives without grumbling and complaining about it? Are we willing to let God choose how He sees fit to bring about our restoration? Will we press on and not give up, so we can let the Lord refine us, even if it means hanging on for dear life at times? I say, "Yes, Lord. Have Your way in my life. Have Your way."

Think about your greatest adversary in life. It is typically the person who rubs you the wrong way. Is there more than one? Think about the ways you feel triggered when you interact with that person. What have they poked inside of you, or where did they "hit a nerve"? Have you considered this is an area in your life that maybe the Lord is using others to touch so He can reveal to you that you need healing in this area? The Lord uses people to refine us, and typically when we feel "poked," it is because something is being exposed that needs to be healed.

Once you have discovered those issues, this gives you an opportunity to have a conversation with the Lord about what the root of this issue is in your life so you can walk through repentance or forgiveness as needed. The Father loves you and wants to see you whole. Healing can be instantaneous, but most of the time we must work through healing in layers.

I must admit I have always wanted to rush through healing or any lesson because I know some of the things God has called me to do. I get excited and want those things for my life now. However, I have learned there is wisdom in letting the Lord take His time. So do not try to rush the process and let the Holy Spirit guide you.

As you walk through this process, forgive those you need to and ask the Lord to help you come to a place where you can pray His blessings over those who have come against you. There is no telling what they have been through in their own lives, and they are just walking and manifesting their own pain as you have done in your own life. Offer grace where you can and set healthy boundaries where you need to.

Day 3

But test everything and hold on to what is good.

—1 Thessalonians 5:21 (ESV)

Be of sober *spirit,* be on the alert. Your adversary, the devil, prowls around like a roaring lion, seeking someone to devour.

—1 Peter 5:8 (NASB)

Have you ever heard of the Saran Wrap ball game? It is typically a game that is played during the holidays. It is where all kinds of treats, prizes, and money are wrapped into a large ball and the players get to unwrap it to win the goodies inside.

One morning, I was reading the book *The Discerner* by James Goll, and I saw a picture of that Saran Wrap ball in my mind as I was reading about how evil spirits can deceive us. One of those methods is wrapping the truth with a lie. Imagine seeing one of these oversized balls filled with candy and seeing a Snickers bar in one of the top layers. Not only is your enemy, Satan, trying to wrap lies around the truth to deceive us, he snickers in the process of it all.

The enemy loves to take a kernel of truth and then wrap it in a lie. There can be this tiny piece of truth that is covered again and again with lies or horrible exaggerations until it grows into this huge thing. It becomes the beginning of an accusation against us, which causes a provocation inside of us to retaliate and/or defend ourselves. If we follow that rabbit trail, it will cause us to lose sight of the truth, and we will wind up in the ditch every time.

Day 3 Reflection

John 10:10 talks about how Satan has come only to steal, kill, and destroy. He is your greatest adversary, not people; however, he does use people to accomplish his will. Can you think of a time in your life that someone brought an accusation against you where it was a truth wrapped in a lie?

Have you participated in any slander or gossip against another individual? If so, did a tiny piece of truth grow and morph into something untrue due to the tactics of the enemy or because you were walking in the flesh?

Ask Him to reveal any situations where you have participated in slandering, gossiping, or lying about other people. It is so important to repent and to close any doors you may have intentionally or unintentionally opened.

Have you believed something about yourself because the enemy took a kernel of truth and twisted it to deceive you into believing something about yourself that was not from the Lord?

Ask the Holy Spirit to reveal to you any time you have been deceived by the enemy or have believed any lies about yourself, even if it started out in truth. One of the greatest tactics of the enemy is to twist everything God has created. He twists things so slightly to where many Christians do not ever realize they are being deceived. Only an individual who is walking in constant communion with the Lord or is seeking His wisdom continuously would know what is not of the Father.

Personal Notes

Day 4

I have been crucified with Christ. It is no longer I
who live, but Christ who lives in me. And the life
I now live in the flesh I live by faith in the Son of
God, who loved me and gave himself for me.

—Galatians 2:20 (ESV)

Whoever finds his life will lose it, and whoever
loses his life for my sake will find it.

—Matthew 10:39 (ESV)

There is a worship song I love so much. At one point in the song, the lead singer says, "Let it cost you." It makes me think of those who have come before me—you know, the people just a few generations ago all the way back to the first followers of Jesus. If you know anything about the disciples, you know being a follower of Jesus is supposed to cost us.

Being a follower of Jesus may cost us time, money, friends, our job, and even our lives. I mean, if it is not costing us, are we even doing it right? If it is not costing us, are we walking out what God has declared over our lives? If it is not costing us, are we a threat to the enemy or his kingdom?

There was this American evangelist in the 1960s and 1970s whose name was Kathryn Kuhlman. She was known for healing and miracles. I watched a recorded service once when she was speaking at Oral Roberts University in 1972. She said God had not given her anything special and He could use any of us in the same way if we are willing to pay the price. She went on to say, "I would lie to you, if I were to tell you the price is cheap."

Satan has completely influenced and infiltrated the church and Christianity to where we no longer resemble what the true church, the *ekklesia* (governing body), was created to be. We have been an eagle that has been defeathered and weakened and cannot soar. It is time to learn how to fly again so we can push back the darkness.

Day 4 Reflection

What a great opportunity to reflect on your relationship with the Father. Each of us has a book written about us in heaven. This book includes what God has declared over our lives and what we were specifically created to do.

Psalm 138:8 talks about how the Lord will work out His plans for your life. However, it takes dying to self and letting go of fleshly desires. It takes a willing heart. It takes radical obedience. It takes coming into agreement with what the Father has written over your life so you can partner with Him to accomplish His will to bring heaven to earth as Matthew 6:10 speaks about.

God can do anything He wants and does not need any of us to accomplish His will. However, because He wants a relationship with you, He wants to use you as His vessel to defeat the enemy and bring heaven to earth. Do you want to walk in God's fullness? Do you want to walk out what He has created you for? Ask the Lord to reveal to you what your portion is regarding what God has called you to do and what the cost is. Are you willing to pay the price no matter the cost?

PERSONAL NOTES

Day 5

If I speak in the tongues of men and of angels, but have
not love, I am a noisy gong or a clanging cymbal. If I
have prophetic powers, and understand all mysteries
and all knowledge, and if I have all faith, so as to
remove mountains, but have not love, I am nothing.
If I give away all I have, and if I deliver up my body
to be burned, but have not love, I gain nothing.

—1 Corinthians 13:1–3 (ESV)

The Lord once gave me a new assignment, and it was one that I was not excited about. To be honest, while I was obedient to the call, I was not willing or joyful about it. It is the hardest thing the Lord had ever called me to do. I was having a very difficult time for many reasons. So I had my associate pastor and some friends come to pray for me, this new assignment, and the surrounding community. During our prayer, a friend of mine saw a penny on the ground, and she picked it up. She gave me the penny and told me to ask the Lord for one thing every day to focus on. The first day I asked the Lord about the "one thing" I needed to focus on, He simply told me to "be love." The next day, I asked again, and I heard the same thing: "be love." I am still hearing the same thing every day, "be love."

Being love is easy when things are running smoothly or when we like the people we are around. However, it can be quite difficult to "be love" in times when we are surrounded by our enemies. It is not easy when we are constantly triggered by something or someone or when we are in a tough season of refinement where we are literally walking across hot coals with bare feet.

I watched a video of the prophet Bob Jones talking about his visitation to heaven and how when you get to heaven, the one question you are asked is, Did you learn to love? I would encourage you to go online, search for the video, and watch it. It seems like being love is such a simple concept. But for many, including myself, it would be so much more satisfying to our flesh to throat punch someone instead of having to be refined where we can love those who are a thorn in our flesh. I completely believe it is the greatest thing we can achieve in our lives, and it is something the broken and lost desperately need to have an encounter with.

<h1 style="text-align: center; font-style: italic;">Day 5 Reflection</h1>

The Father has called us all to "be love," because it is the greatest assignment in all our lives. What a great day to ask the Lord to reveal to you the times you have been unloving to others. It does not matter whether you feel they deserve to be loved or not. Everyone is responsible and accountable for their own behavior. If you desire to walk in forgiveness, freedom, and carry the authority of God, those issues must be dealt with to become a holy vessel used for God's glory.

If you have been unloving to others, free yourself and those you have not loved well through repentance. Ask the Lord to release you from any consequences of the times you did not walk in love. Ask Him to reveal to you the root of why you might be unloving. Is it a generational iniquity you were born with or something you opened the door to in your life? Are you unloving all the time? Is it just toward specific people? Is it just during those stressful or triggering times? Those are the times that our true character is revealed. Then ask Him to give you His heart for people.

I believe these are ongoing issues that everyone faces. Healing and refinement come in layers as you continuously pursue Jesus and die to self. There is no condemnation or shame in it, just freedom and restoration if you are willing to put in the work.

<u>PERSONAL NOTES</u>

Day 6

Behold, I give you authority to trample on serpents
and scorpions, and authority over all the power
of the enemy, and nothing will injure you.

—Luke 10:19 (NASB)

And let us not grow weary in doing good, for in
due season we will reap, if we do not give up.

—Galatians 6:9 (ESV)

One day the Lord spoke to me and said, "The spiritual authority I have given you is greater than any battle you will face. Rise up, o' daughter." When I was younger, I felt fearless as if I could take on almost anything. Sometimes I was quite reckless, and being fearless would get me into a bit of trouble every now and then.

As I have gotten older and have been through many difficult seasons one after another, I have become weary. There have been many times I have wanted to give up and throw in the towel. It is during those times I have had to reach out to my spiritual family for strength, encouragement, and a word from the Lord to keep pressing on.

It is not easy to constantly be in a season of warring, training, or testing. When one battle ends, the next one begins, and all you wish for is just a little break or time of peace in between battles. What I have learned about these seasons is that they are vital to my becoming who the Lord created me to be. These seasons have made me become a serious weightlifter in the spirit. I have even been told by several people that I am very large and weighty in the spirit, which is exciting and yet makes me chuckle a bit when I think about it. God really is the coolest. It is a shame that many people think God is boring. Religion might be boring, but I assure you having a relationship with the Father is anything but dull.

So, when the Lord spoke to me the spiritual authority I have is greater than any battle I will face, He was saying that I have the tools to win the battle and I need to stand up and actively use what I have already been given. I have already overcome because I walk from a place of victory to victory, and it is because He is my Champion and Defender. I just have to walk it out and remember everything I need, He has already put it inside of me.

I hope today was especially encouraging to you. God has given us great authority over the enemy. He has already put inside of us everything we would need to achieve His purposes and plans for our lives. We just have to desire to be willing and obedient and to partner with Him to bring His kingdom to earth. Today, I would encourage you to begin a conversation about how He wants to use you to bring heaven to earth.

My friend Karen has taught me three great questions to ask the Lord:

- Lord, what are You doing?
- Lord, what do You want me to know?
- Lord, what is my portion in this? (Sometimes your portion is to just pray and release it, and other times it is getting involved. It is just very important not to carry burdens that the Lord did not ask us to carry.)

You can ask the Lord these questions anytime you feel a prompting about any situation or topic. For example, it could be about something going on with a friend, politics or governmental issues, a natural disaster, or something going on in your own life or sphere of influence. Just allow the

Holy Spirit to guide you in all things and pray for the revelation you need and then be obedient to what the Lord calls you to do next.

As time continues, the goal is to spiritually look better than Arnold Schwarzenegger in his prime. We are going to need to be mighty in the spirit to deal with what is coming in the future.

Day 7

Go, therefore, and make disciples of all the nations,
baptizing them in the name of the Father, and
the Son, and the Holy Spirit, teaching them to
follow all that I commanded you; and behold I
am with you always, to the end of the age.

—Matthew 28:19–20 (NASB)

Sometimes you just do not want to walk into the darkness and deal with all the people who have serious issues or demons. Then you remember that person was once you.

I grew up in church but turned my back on God and rebelliously chose to walk in the way I had wanted for many years. I felt religion was so full of too many legalistic rules that I was never going to be able to fulfill, so why bother? Yet, like so many other people, I categorized myself as a Christian because I believed in God but had no relationship with Him.

After decades of walking in severe depravity and darkness, the Lord gave me a dream that scared the literal hell out of me. In this dream, He showed me that demons were dancing around a bonfire celebrating I was going to hell. The King of all heaven and earth loved me so much that He left the ninety-nine to find his lost sheep, his daughter (Matthew 18:12), by speaking to me when I was asleep to get my attention—all because I refused to listen to Him while I was awake.

The Lord has cleaned me up where I no longer feel darkness running through my veins. He has physically healed me, He has spiritually healed me, and He continues to walk me through restoration to this day. So, with all the goodness and mercy the Lord has shown me, how can I not extend that to others if the Lord is calling me to them? I do not know about you, but I do not want any person to spend their eternity in hell, and I want to receive my rewards in heaven for walking out what God has called me to do.

He has called us all to be His servant, His light, to be the salt of the earth, to worship and praise Him, and to partner with Him to see His will manifest on the earth. But He also gave us a commandment, not a request, to help pull people out of darkness. If we will allow God to use us, people can have their own life-changing encounters with Jesus.

Day 7 Reflection

I want you to think about your own story of salvation today. Maybe you have always served the Lord. If so, that is wonderful. If your testimony is one that took a divine intervention and was miraculous, that is wonderful too.

However, are you accepting the mandate to go into all the nations and bring people into the kingdom? If you have not at this point, there is no condemnation in Christ Jesus (Romans 8:1). However, Matthew 28:19–20 was not a request; it was a command. It was a directive not given to just a chosen few, but it was given to everyone so the kingdom can grow and advance. Going to the nations does not mean you have to go abroad. If you will just look around you in your own city or town, at every turn you will see the face of someone who represents the nations.

I encourage you to be compassionate to others and help pull them out of the darkness as the Lord did for you. The harvest is there for the taking, especially if we are letting the Lord guide us to those He wants to touch in the current season. Now go out there and let your light shine for the kingdom.

Day 8

Do not be conformed to this world, but be
transformed by the renewing of your mind, that
by testing you may discern what is the will of God,
what is good, and acceptable, and perfect.

—Romans 12:2 (ESV)

Put on the full armor of God, so that you will be able
to stand firm against the schemes of the devil.

—Ephesians 6:11 (NASB)

It is funny how the Lord will speak to you in so many ways and at such random times if you are willing to hear what He has to say. One day I was looking at my landscaping in the front of my house. Just three weeks prior, it was weed- and grass-free. All the pine straw had been removed, and my husband and I were waiting to figure out what we were going to do because of a drainage situation.

As I was looking at my flower beds, I realized it did not take long for grass and weeds to settle in. It is crazy how fast weeds begin to grow, especially when you are not using any type of weed prevention. The next thing you know, you have a very ugly and embarrassing situation on your hands.

Our relationship with the Lord is the same way. Our lives can grow weeds and can get out of hand quick if we are not tending to our spiritual landscaping every day and throughout each day.

Having a relationship with the Lord will be the most beautiful and delightful experience of your life. The more I pursue Him, the deeper our relationship becomes. It never feels like a burden or something I must do to prevent going to hell. It feels like every part of my being was made to be with Him, to know Him and be known by Him, to love and worship Him, and to be loved by Him. Being in the presence of the Father makes me melt, and it has made my spiritual landscape become lush and beautiful because of every encounter I have with Him.

Day 8 Reflection

Have you left yourself vulnerable to attacks from the enemy by not putting on your armor every day? Have you given a foothold to the enemy in your mind or life because you are not renewing your mind with the Word of God daily? Are you spending time with the Father in the secret place? For in His presence is where you will find joy, strength, peace, and revelation. If you are not spending time with the Father, please do not let yourself step into condemnation or judgment over it. However, it is not safe or beneficial for you to remain in the place you currently are.

Today is a good day to begin spending time forming a deeper relationship with the Father. He greatly desires for you to get to know Him and learn what He thinks and says about you. He also wants to dote on you and love you like a good father because He is such a good Father.

Ask the Lord to reveal to you what it means to be in the secret place with Him. If you struggle finding time or have difficulty focusing, ask Him to help you in this area. You would not be the first person or the last to have this struggle.

As you walk out today, study the armor of God and what each piece represents and what it is used for. Then begin to put on your armor every day to protect yourself from the fiery darts of the enemy.

Personal Notes

Day 9

Consider it all joy, my brothers and sisters, when
you encounter various trials, knowing that the
testing of your faith produces endurance.

—James 1:2–3 (NASB)

Do all things without complaining or arguments.

—Philippians 2:14 (NASB)

I abhor injustice, true injustice. My name even means
"judge." I have always stood against injustice. I have
fought for the underdog and have laid myself on the altar
many times over injustice. I know that in most of those situations I did not deal with injustice God's way.

It makes me think about Moses because of the Egypt
and Pharaoh issues our society is plagued with today. When I
think about Moses, initially I think about the Red Sea being
parted, or I think about him throwing the staff on the ground
and it becomes a serpent. But, before all that, Moses was a
guy who dealt with injustice in an improper way, and he had
to flee into the wilderness over it.

Sometimes we need to flee into the wilderness to protect our future. In the wilderness, we go through testing and training imperative for our spiritual growth. During these seasons, we can feel alone and abandoned, and it can be hard to feel God's presence or even hear His voice. However, I assure you we are not alone, not there, not ever. The Father gave us Jesus and the Holy Spirit, so we are never alone.

It is important to count it all joy and not step into a place of complaining during our times in the wilderness. Those types of attitudes can lengthen our stay. So give thanks! The wilderness is like a spiritual boot camp of overcoming, which is something the enemy cannot stand. So he will come at us repeatedly because he fears our victory. We can walk in the same authority and victory as Moses or anyone else. There is not anything that God has done for anyone in the Bible that He will not do for us. However, before we can lead a people, we must learn how to yield ourselves to those seasons in the wilderness and be thankful for them. Even Jesus spent time in the wilderness and was tested (Matthew 4:1).

I give you an invitation today to have a conversation with the Father about the wilderness and what it really means to be set apart in a wilderness season. Have you felt like you were in a barren and dry season? Have you cried out and wondered, *God, where are You?* Ask for Jesus to show you where He is during those times. I have no doubt He is standing right next to you walking with you at every step in the wilderness even when you cannot feel Him. This is typically when He is doing the most work on your behalf, when you feel Him the least. You are not alone and never have been, not one single day of your life.

I know the wilderness can be quite uncomfortable and even painful. But, beloved, the pain is considered productive pain, and it refines and prepares you for what lies ahead in your journey. It is the act of a loving and kind Father to take you through the wilderness so you can come out with the ability to withstand the enemy and walk in victory.

To be honest, there is more to the wilderness than we understand. We may perceive the wilderness to be a dry and barren place, but it is not. It is possible we have this misperception because of how uncomfortable it feels to be in a wilderness season. It was in the wilderness that the Israelites were provided manna. It was in the wilderness that Jesus was given the tools to defeat Satan. Beloved, in the wilderness, there is a hidden oasis of provision in the natural and in the spirit. Do not let the enemy fool you into thinking otherwise.

If you have been resistant or have complained about being in the wilderness, I would encourage you to repent. Ask the Lord to forgive you and to continue refining you. Ask Him to bring you into alignment in any area you are not aligned with Him. Then give thanks and watch what He does in your life as you continue to submit to Him with a joyful heart.

Personal Notes

Day 10

Heal the sick, raise the dead, cleanse those with leprosy,
cast out demons. Freely you have received, freely give.

—Matthew 10:8 (NASB)

And He said to them, "Go into all the world
and preach the gospel to all creation."

—Mark 16:15 (NASB)

I was the very person who needed massive healing and deliverance when I came to the Lord. Although I had been going to church for years, I was not bearing any real fruit as a Christian. On the outside I looked like any other Christian though. I was involved. I was on teams, leading teams, and even leading Bible studies. However, on the inside I was a mess! I was still broken. There was not one person I trusted, secretly not even my husband. I could not read the Bible without falling asleep, and I had no real relationship with the Lord. I did not know how, and it was because for me to begin receiving from the Lord, I needed major healing and deliverance.

I eventually found a church who understood that the mandate of Jesus was more than just saving souls and surface-level Christianity. This ministry understood the entire mandate of Jesus and believes the whole Word. They accepted the full mandate, even the messy parts, which include deliverance, getting healed of deep wounds, physical healing, the prophetic, and allowing the Holy Spirit to always be in the lead of everything that happens. Many churches avoid deliverance, the prophetic, and even allowing the Holy Spirit to have complete control of the service. I understand why, because if those things are not shepherded well, it could not only be messy but disastrous. However, these things are not an option; they are a mandate from the Lord.

At this point, I have received a major amount of healing and deliverance. To see the person I have become and am still becoming is quite beautiful. Healing and deliverance never ends, and I always get excited when I realize another part of me that was not pleasing to the Lord has been removed due to my willingness to let the Lord have His way with me. I have also received quite a bit of physical healing along the way. I have been healed from torment of the mind, vertigo, and several other things. Now, I pray and help lead others through their own life struggles and healing. It is very humbling. As I write this, I am crying because I never thought the Lord could use me in such a way.

Day 10 Reflection

There is much more to the gospel than just saving souls. Yet, if we are only focusing on saving souls, this is only part of the mandate of Jesus. What happens if we focus only on saving souls? What happens to the newly saved person once they have accepted Jesus as their Lord and Savior? A person may come into the flock, but do they know how to work out their salvation (Philippians 2:12)? This is not just a "one and done" process. Once a person chooses to become a follower of Jesus, this person most likely needs healing and deliverance at some level. We cannot bring people to Jesus and leave them to walk through life spiritually, emotionally, and physically crippled. We cannot leave people in a place where they feel ill prepared to face the natural and spiritual battles in their lives once they are saved.

Today, I want you to think about where you are personally with the Lord. Are you hungry for the deeper things of God? Do you need healing and deliverance from something? Are you walking out the mandates of Jesus to preach the gospel and to bring healing and deliverance to others? Let this day be just the beginning of a conversation of all those things.

You can ask the Lord to give you a deeper revelation of Him and to take you to higher places. You can ask the Lord about an area you are struggling in which you need healing.

I will say, if you have a need for physical healing, most of the time, it is because there is a spiritual root that must be dealt with, such as bitterness, unforgiveness, fear, self-hate, pride, etc. Ask the Lord to show you the root of what you are dealing with, whether it be a physical or inner healing issue. If you need to repent, be quick to do so, and do not allow yourself to step into shame or condemnation over it. Shame and condemnation are not from the Lord; they are tools used by the enemy to keep us in shackles.

Then ask the Lord how you can go out into the world (which may be your very city or perhaps it is to the nations) and walk out the mandates He has given to us all to preach the gospel, bring healing to the sick, and help others become free from demonic oppression. The Holy Spirit is always there to guide you. If you are not baptized in the Holy Spirit, what a great opportunity for you to ask the Father to baptize you at this very moment. How excited I am for you, beloved.

Day 11

For the wages of sin is death, but the free gift of
God is eternal life in Christ Jesus our Lord.

—Romans 6:23 (ESV)

Some were fools through their sinful ways, and
because of their iniquities, suffered affliction.

—Psalm 107:17 (ESV)

Have you ever heard the statement *This runs in my family?* Have you ever looked at your family tree and seen the pattern of issues that your family has consistently dealt with? It could be a behavior, a mindset, or even a health condition. When I first started walking through healing and deliverance, I thought about my family tree. When I looked at my family history, I immediately saw multiple generations dealing with the same junk. I saw divorce, addiction, fornication, adultery, manipulation, anger, and many other sins that have run rampant in my family. My father and my mother's father both died very tragic deaths. Other people might recognize more physical conditions in their family tree, such as multiple generations dying from a heart attack or brain tumors. All these types of issues are called generational curses or iniquities.

This may challenge your current belief system, but the Lord did not create anything to "run in our family." He created us to walk in relationship with Him and to be at full strength until the day He calls us home. Yet, because of separation from God, it causes sin to creep in. And we put our very lives at risk to that which causes illness, mental health issues, and even early death.

While all these issues stem from sin in our lives, it is not always sin you personally committed. We are born into sin, so it could be sin that has been passed down through your bloodline to you and even your children. There are certain unclean spirits called familiar spirits that will study our family, find open doors so they can have legal access to our bloodlines, and have access to the next generation to instigate death and destruction over their lives. They are very tricky because we often give these familiar spirits access to our lives innocently because it feels familiar and comfortable to us.

If we want to walk in freedom, we must be willing to deal with those iniquities. This comes through repenting not only for us but for our entire bloodline, all the way back to Adam. Repentance is the only way, unless God performs a miracle, to cleanse our bloodlines from the curses of sin that plague our families. He wants to free us from the consequences of being separated from Him, but we have to be willing and desire to put in the work.

Today it is important to reflect on any sin in your life and what might have been passed down to you from your ancestors, even many generations ago. There is no telling what kind of iniquities might be in your bloodline that happened centuries ago. The best place to start is asking the Holy Spirit to show you.

I have known many people who have had conversations with the Lord, and the Holy Spirit has revealed some very dark and hidden iniquities passed down their bloodline. The Lord wants to reveal those things to you to break the chains of bondage in your family tree. You might be the only individual who now has the knowledge about generational iniquities, and you could be the very person the Lord wants to use to help set your bloodline free.

The Father is good, and He is not going to throw some huge list at you so He can throw the book at you. He may only present one area to focus on at a time. I know we want to be restored and healed and we want it now. However, healing and deliverance takes time, and there are often layers that must be peeled off one at a time. The work is totally worth it, so hang in there even when you feel frustrated.

Day 12

Keep me as the apple of your eye, hide
me in the shadow of your wings.

—Psalm 17:8 (ESV)

The Lord your God is in your midst, a mighty
one who will save; he will rejoice over you with
gladness; He will quiet you with His love, He
will rejoice over you with loud singing.

—Zephaniah 3:17 (ESV)

Before I formed you in the womb I knew you,
and before you were born I consecrated you; I
appointed you a prophet to the nations.

—Jeremiah 1:5 (ESV)

I feel like the Lord wanted today to be all about how much He loves you. He knew you before He knit you together in your mother's womb. He wants you to know that you are precious to Him. You are the apple of His eye, and He sings over you, beloved.

I do not know what your life is like or what you have gone through. You may feel unworthy or undeserving of the Father's love. Guess what? We all are, but it is because of the blood of Jesus that we have become worthy. Perhaps you have never felt loved, approved of, or valuable to anyone. *You* are valuable to the Father. *You* are His prize possession. He loves you so much that He would send Jesus into the world to be born as a man. The very same man died for your sins so you could live in relationship with the Father. *You* are not rejected, *you* are not abandoned, and *you* are a blessing. There is nothing that can separate you from the love of God (Romans 8:38–39).

The Father, Jesus, and Holy Spirit long to be with you and walk in constant communion with you. They deeply desire to have an intimate relationship with you, one where there are no walls or veils between you. I believe sometimes we know this in our heads, but we do not understand this love in our hearts.

While you may love God greatly, it is also important you learn to receive love. Stop running from His love, my friend. The Father is waiting to shower you with a love like you have never experienced and will only encounter with Him.

Day 12 Reflection

If you struggle with feeling loved or receiving love, I encourage you to ask the Lord to show you the root of why you feel that way. Maybe there is something that happened in your life that hurt you so deeply and it left you wounded. These wounds, if left unhealed, leave cracks for the enemy to enter and have legal right to oppress us.

Right now, the Lord just showed me that some of you are carrying around these humongous bags of hurt and pain. You have believed a lie or lies somewhere and made an agreement with those lies. Now they have become a part of who you believe you are. It is not who you are, and it is important to begin the healing process so you can learn who you are in Christ Jesus and be able to receive and give love freely.

Once the Lord has shown you the root of why you have difficulty feeling, giving, or receiving love, it is important that you repent for any lies you have believed. Break agreement with those lies and then ask the Lord to remove any consequences in the natural and in the spirit from aligning with things that are not from the Lord. Any type of healing and deliverance can happen all at once, but I do want to remind you most of the time healing comes in layers. We walk through healing, but another layer of junk is often revealed and a deeper level of healing is needed. The Father is gentle, so allow the Holy Spirit to guide you through this.

Do not be quick to rush through healing because the Father wants to deal with healing in His time at His pace. He knows exactly what you need and wants what is best for you. Trust the process.

I would like to end today's reflection with a prayer over you, beloved.

Father, I pray over every person who is reading this. I know with You all things are possible, and so I pray Your children will be able to receive what You have for them today. I pray that You overwhelm them with Your presence and Your love. I pray You begin to shatter every lie Your precious child has believed that has left them feeling unloved, rejected, abandoned, or unable to give and receive love. I pray You will tear down every brick of every wall Your beloved has built out of fear or to protect themselves from further pain. I declare Your goodness will be made known to them so they will begin to see You and the depths of Your love for them. I come into agreement with what You have spoken over their life, and they would know they were created for good works and You delight in them.

Father, I thank You for what You are doing right now in the life of the child You love endlessly. I give You all the glory, all the honor, and all the praise. In the mighty name of Jesus. Amen.

Day 13

The Spirit of the Lord spoke through me,
and his word was on my tongue.

—2 Samuel 23:2 (NASB)

For you can all prophesy one by one, so that
all may learn and all be encouraged.

—1 Corinthians 14:31 (ESV)

The Lord is always speaking to us. He uses Scripture, songs, other people, dreams, visions, and all of creation to grasp our attention and speak to us. He is always trying to communicate and be in relationship with us. I openly admit there was a time in my life when I kept on saying, "But I cannot hear the Lord." While I did need some deliverance to be able to hear the Lord, I also needed to stop declaring that I could not hear the Lord. I was cursing myself! I also needed to position myself in a place where I could practice hearing the Lord in the ways He chooses to speak to me. Sometimes it is during praise and worship through lyrics. Sometimes it is when I am doing yard work or cleaning that I get a word. Sometimes I get a picture in my mind's eye, and I know it is from the Lord. A lot of the Lord's communication with me is in my dreams. Sometimes the Father communicates something specific to me from Scripture, sometimes through a movie I am watching, and often He communicates to me through others in what is known as prophecy. I absolutely love the gift of prophecy!

Without hearing the words that God has spoken over our lives before we were ever born, we do not get the direction we need to walk out what the Father created us for. Overall, prophetic words can give directions for cities or nations and show us what is coming to prepare or know what to pray. The prophetic helps us see the assignment of the enemy and know what season we are walking in, how to speak into people's lives to bring them freedom and encouragement, and so much more. It is vital for the body of Christ to be open to the prophetic so we can hear what God wants us to know so we can partner with Him for His will to be accomplished in our lives and on the earth.

For me personally, prophetic ministry has given me the opportunity for reconciliation with the Lord. It has led me to repentance, helped me heal, brought me edification, and given me insight to know what the Lord is wanting me to do in different seasons of my life. The use of prophecy has shown me how God sees me and how much He thinks I am His favorite (you are too). And, due to some specific prophetic words that have been given to me, it confirmed a dream I had in my heart as a child was not just a dream; it was what God purposely put inside me to accomplish in my life.

<h1 style="text-align:center">Day 13 Reflection</h1>

Beloved, in many circles of Christianity, people do not believe in the gift of prophecy. However, the New Testament talks about it. I want you to get excited, because not only does God speak to us but He gives everyone the ability to prophesy. No, not everyone is a prophet, but 1 Corinthians 14:31 says all may prophesy. Some might be prophets, but there are other levels of the gift of prophecy.

Today is a great day to reflect on any ideas, beliefs you may have, or any misconceptions you may have about the prophetic. Yes, it can seem mysterious, but sometimes we cannot fathom something we do not quite understand or have not learned yet. Perhaps your church does not speak about it, so you are not sure what to think about it. I would encourage you to investigate it for yourself. If you look in 1 Corinthians 12:7–11, it talks about the different gifts of the spirit we have access to. The gift of prophecy is one of those. And we are supposed to greatly desire all these gifts, especially the gift of prophecy (1 Corinthians 14:1).

My friend, if you have believed any lies about the prophetic, I would encourage you to have a conversation with the Lord to see what He says about it. If you struggle to believe prophecy is real or are not sure if it is still for today, ask the Lord to give you the faith to believe. If you want to move in the gift of prophecy, ask the Lord for it. If you do not have anyone around you to help mentor you in using prophecy as God intended, there are some great resources online that can teach you. They will not only teach you about how to hear the Lord and how to prophesy but also teach you to be cautious of prophesying from your soul, which is a big no-no. One of my favorite ministries is Streams International, which John Paul Jackson founded before he passed away. He had great prophetic insight, especially in dream interpretation. One of my favorite authors regarding prophecy is Graham Cooke. He has a multitude of resources, and I encourage you to check him out.

I pray today that the Father is stirring up something inside of you that will give you a hunger for every gift He wants to give you, especially the gift of prophecy. My spirit is so excited for you as you search out the things of God. Just remember, beloved, let your first love always be the Father and not the gifts He gives. Sometimes we can lose focus and get caught up in the amazing aspects of the gifts if we are not careful, and it can move us into a place where we are using the Lord for what He can give us, instead of loving Him solely because He is our Father.

Personal Notes

<h1 style="text-align:center">Day 14</h1>

He heals the brokenhearted and binds up their wounds.

—Psalm 147:3 (ESV)

When I was a little girl, I loved riding my bike as fast as I could down the sloped street we lived on. One day, I rode that bike with all my might and accidentally hit a pothole on the side of the street. I flipped off my bike and landed on the road, which caused me to get gravel stuck in my skin right underneath my chin. I remember my pawpaw coming to my rescue, picking me up, and carrying me into the house to take care of me.

Every time I see those two little scars under my chin, I am not only reminded of how much my pawpaw loved me, but I am reminded of how the love he showed me as a child is a beautiful reflection of how my Father feels about me every second of every single day.

When we are at our best or at our worst, our Father still loves us. When we get distracted by other things and lose our focus on Him, He still loves us. When we get angry and frustrated, become disobedient, and want to give up, He still loves us. God is always trying to draw us back to Himself because we are His children and, like a good father, He also wants to heal our broken heart and bind up our wounds.

Day 14 Reflection

Friend, life can be so painful. Not one person is immune from feeling hurt and frustrated, loss, disappointment, rejection, abandonment, sadness, or feelings of depression. I openly admit I have felt all those feelings and more. Beloved, I am truly sorry if you have ever felt any of those things in your life. I am sorry for all times someone has hurt you, intentionally or unintentionally.

Today, I want you to know that your Father loves you so much. He is waiting for you to run into His arms and sit in His lap. Can you envision that? Try to see yourself sitting in the Father's lap while He is holding you. Tell Him about your hurts. Although He already knows you better than you know yourself, He is a good Father, and He is waiting and ready to listen to you. Share your heart with Him.

You do not have to unload everything in one sitting. Take your time and let the Holy Spirit guide you. If you see a specific memory that caused you pain, start with that. If you want to start with a feeling, such as rejection, ask the Holy Spirit to show you when the seed of rejection was first planted in your life. Then you can ask Jesus where He was during that situation. He will show you where He was, and you will know that He has always been there with you.

As you are walking through your hurts with the Lord, it is possible that you might need to repent for something the

Lord has revealed to you or that you might need to forgive someone. You may not be ready to forgive just yet. If you do not feel ready to forgive, ask the Lord to help you become ready to forgive and then to help you forgive. You cannot do this on your own. If you refuse to forgive, please understand the person who is most held captive by unforgiveness is you. It imprisons you in ways you may never realize. Many times, the person we need to forgive does not even know of their offense toward us.

Forgiveness is important. While it does not take away the action that took place that caused the pain, it allows the sting of what happened to be removed. It also frees you and your offender from being held captive. Sometimes the person we need to forgive most is ourselves.

The Bible mandates that we forgive (Ephesians 4:32). We have been forgiven much, so we must come to a place where we can forgive freely as well. You already know healing and deliverance takes time; forgiveness may take time as well. As you allow the Father to heal your wounds, eventually you will come to a place where you can let go of the hurts and trauma that has taken place in your life. What a great journey this will be for you to find restoration. I am excited for you, friend!

<u>Personal Notes</u>

Day 15

Draw near to God, and he will draw near to you.

—James 4:8 (ESV)

But as for me, the nearness of God is good
for me; I have made the Lord God my refuge.
So that I may tell of all Your works.

—Psalm 73:28 (NASB)

I always felt that I had this great calling on my life to do big things, but time and time again I would become more derailed from that calling due to poor choices I had made. My flesh was in the driver's seat; and my choices were based on a feeling of unworthiness, rebellion, pride, brokenness, and lust.

One of my biggest mistakes was rejecting God and His ways while calling myself a Christian. I will openly admit I was completely turned off by religion. What I did not understand is there is a difference between being religious and being in relationship with the Lord. Go back and read the Bible where it talks about the Pharisees and the Sadducees. Those were religious people; those were the very people who hated Jesus when He stepped onto the scene. Those were the people so focused on keeping to the rules of religion and doing "works." They were always judging and greatly desired the punishment of individuals for not obeying the rules.

What I have come to realize is that the Father is looking to be in a relationship with us. He is looking for a true love affair, one where we are in constant communion with Him. He is looking for individuals who will set themselves apart in the secret place and only be with Him. The Father is not looking for loyal subjects or minions to control. He is looking for people who will willingly submit themselves to Him so He can transform their lives and walk in oneness with Him. He is looking for those who will die to their own desires and take up the calling He has written over their lives before they were born. He also wants to partner with us to bring heaven to earth (Matthew 6:10).

I realized throughout my life I have had some serious misconceptions about God and I did not understand Him at all or His ways. We often feel about God the same way we do about our natural father, and if we did not have a good father in life, it can be difficult to see God as a loving Father. However, I promise you God is not only a good God but He is also a very good Father. He is just waiting for you to say yes to Him so He can begin to show you the depths of His love, heal and restore you, and train you so you can take your rightful place in the kingdom. He needs you!

Day 15 Reflection

Today, I want to come before you and stand in the place of the church or anyone who misrepresented God to you in any way. As I stand on their behalf, I want to repent for any time you have been hurt by the church, by people proclaiming to be religious, or by anyone who represented God in a wrongful manner.

Beloved, I am deeply sorry I have wounded you and caused you any pain, whether it was intentional or unintentional. I repent for misrepresenting the Father to you; it is not the Father who lacks but I who have lacked understanding of who the Father is and who I am called to be as His child.

I repent for any of the ways I have abused you, abused your trust, and deceived you. I repent for not showing you the love of the Father and for not walking in His truth and being a light for His kingdom. I repent for any time I have shunned you, excluded you, and made you feel condemned. I repent for ignoring your cries for help when you needed to have an encounter with the Father through me.

You are His priceless treasure. You are loved and sought after by Him. There is no excuse for the hurt I have caused you, but it is my deepest desire to repent and that you be released from the wounds I have inflicted upon you.

Friend, I know the Lord deeply desires for you to forgive so you can be made whole. He is waiting for you to come home to Him where you belong, where you have always belonged. I pray you will earnestly seek Him so the healing process can begin.

Note: What we just walked through is called identification repentance. This is where an individual can stand in and represent a specific individual or group and repent to you on their behalf.

Day 16

For I have not spoken in my own authority, but
the Father who sent me has himself given me a
commandment—what to say and what to speak.

—John 12:49 (ESV)

So Jesus said to them, "Truly, truly, I say to you,
the son can do nothing of his own accord, but
only what he sees the Father doing. For whatever
the Father does, that the Son does likewise."

—John 5:19 (ESV)

The world is so full of opinions and sayings of what we now call "my truth." I grew up in a very opinionated household, and as I became an adult, I was very opinionated. I would freely share my opinion whether I was asked or not. Along with that came a need to be right. I really believe those character traits walk hand in hand.

However, if we are not just believers in Jesus but followers of Jesus, we are called to die to self and become one with Him (Galatians 2:20). This involves submitting our tongues to the Father and asking Him to purify our tongues. It is not an easy process to walk through, but with God all things are possible (Mark 10:27).

When we submit our tongues to the Father and we fight against our flesh to be one with Jesus, our opinions seem to become less relevant. Please understand I am not referring to having an opinion over which restaurant you like better, like Whataburger vs. In-N-Out Burger. I am referring to having opinions over people, situations, politics, etc. We know according to Proverbs 18:2, there is the power of life and death in the tongue. Therefore, it is important for us to submit our tongues to the Lord, especially when it comes to opinions or even cursing someone with our words. I will talk about word curses on a different day.

When we speak out opinions about any individual or any situation, when it flows out of our mouths, it sets something into motion in the spirit and in the natural. There are consequences for it, either good or bad. If you read the verses for the day at the top, you will know that Jesus only spoke and did what the Father said. To become one with Jesus, we have the same mandate. The mandate is not what we think about a situation or person; it is about what God says about that person or situation. Then we ask Him questions like "What do You want me to speak aloud about that situation or individual?"

Our greatest desire in life in our journey to become more like Jesus is to only do and say what the Father wants us to do and speak. This is life-giving and no doubt will bring heaven to earth.

Beloved, we are all guilty of speaking our opinions or "our truth" into situations and the lives of others. However, the only truth is God's truth, and His truth is unrivaled. Anything other than that is irrelevant.

Today, I would ask you to repent for all the times you have spoken out against something or someone that was unnecessary, was not life-giving, and was not in alignment with God's thoughts. I would encourage you to submit yourselves to the Lord and ask Him to purify your tongue and your heart. Ask the Father to teach you to use your tongue wisely and to speak what He wants you to speak when He wants you to speak. What comes forth from your mouth, you give life to. We do not want to give life to things that are not from God.

Unfortunately, it will be a battle you may always struggle against. Our tongue is a great weapon, one that we will use to bring death and destruction or life. We all struggle with taming of the tongue; so please do not feel condemned. It is tough training, but I know you are an overcomer because of the blood of Jesus.

Day 17

Death and life are in the power of the tongue, And
those who love it and indulge in it will eat its fruit
and bear the consequences of their words.

—Proverbs 18:21 (AMP)

One who guards his mouth protects his life; One
who opens wide his lips comes to ruin.

—Proverbs 13:3 (NASB)

There is one whose rash words are like sword thrusts,
but the tongue of the wise brings healing.

—Proverbs 12:18 (ESV)

Today we will continue with the topic of taming the
tongue as I share revelation about word curses. A word
curse is the opposite of blessing. When a word curse is spoken
over someone, that is a word spoken against someone that
does not line up with the Word of God or what the Father
has spoken over us. A word curse is not some hocus-pocus
where a witch has cast a spell over you. However, I must
tell you it is equal to the same thing. Yet, as Christians, we

often speak word curses over people or situations all the time, whether intentionally or unintentionally.

Now, I will continue to say this: there is no condemnation in Christ Jesus. Please do not allow the enemy to put shame or condemnation on you. We have all fallen short and need the grace of Jesus to wash over us and cleanse us of our unrighteousness. But I want you to understand how simple it is to curse someone with our tongues and the power that those curses have over that person, a situation, and you as well.

Imagine as your child is growing up, they have difficulty seeing the positive in any situation. Imagine them focusing on what they do not have instead of being thankful for what they have. Then imagine the Lord revealing to you that when your child was little, you spoke over their life and told them how ungrateful they were and how they never appreciated anything. Friends, that person was me. I unintentionally cursed my child out of my own frustration and brokenness. Although I know I am forgiven, I still want to cry when I think about how I had once spoken curses over the people I love.

Words are extremely powerful, and when we curse someone, we also curse ourselves. Picture a man who criticizes his wife for her cooking and then his wife becomes depressed and so she stops cooking. The husband who has word cursed her will also reap from cursing her. For example, it could cause him to suddenly develop some type of gastrointestinal or stomach issues. Friends, word curses are very real, and we must guard our tongues.

Today, I want you to think about any words that you may have spoken, whether intentional or not, that may have brought a curse over someone, a situation in your own life, or yourself. I would encourage you to grab a pen and some paper because you may need to write down what the Lord reveals to you or perhaps what you already know in your heart.

Is there anywhere you have cursed yourself? Have you called yourself ugly? Have you said things like "I will never lose weight" or "I will never get married" when you have a deep desire to lose weight or be married? Write down what you have spoken about yourself to repent for cursing yourself.

Have you cursed others, whether it be someone you personally know or someone you do not know, such as the president? Oh, I know that one has inflamed some of you. However, word curses apply to all words you have spoken aloud about all people you have spoken them over. We are all guilty of saying those kinds of things. However, the Lord wants us to be restored and walk in freedom from bondage. So walking through this is a very important process.

Have you cursed your family members? Have you spoken things over your spouse or children that do not line up with the Word of God? I am going to be frank with you and say curses can be as simple as you calling your child a "little turd." These things can be spoken in anger, frustration, or even a teasing manner. It does not matter the intention; once they are spoken aloud, life is given to those words.

As you are writing these things down, repent for what you need to and then ask the Lord to release the person and yourself from the consequences of the curse that was spoken.

Also, today is a good time to remember any word curses that have been spoken over us. We must repent for believing those lies, and we must break agreement with them. As you go through this process, it is important to forgive the person who spoke the word curses over you so it can release you both from the bondage those curses have held you in.

I am so excited for you as you walk through this. Remember healing and forgiveness comes in layers. Let the Holy Spirit oversee your journey. He knows what you can deal with in your current season and what needs to wait until another time. The goal is always restoration in His time.

Be blessed and know the Father has already won the battle for you.

Personal Notes

Day 18

My son, pay attention to my words; incline
your ears to my sayings. They are not to escape
from your sight; Keep them in the midst of
your heart. For they are life to those who
find them, And healing to all their body.

—Proverbs 4:20–22 (NASB)

But put on the Lord Jesus Christ, and make no
provision for the flesh, to gratify its desires.

—Romans 13:14 (ESV)

As far back as I can remember, I have had a passion for two things, music from every genre and writing. Both have always been therapeutic and the source of great satisfaction. As an adolescent, I remember putting my head in between the two speakers of my stereo and getting lost in the lyrics. I would also spend a lot of time writing poetry and short stories.

A few years ago, I was taking a class with Jon, one of the associate pastors at my church. He began talking about the origin of the word *music*. It comes from the Greek word *muse*, and the word *muse* means "to meditate on or be absorbed in thought."

If I am listening to music, it means I am listening to another individual's thoughts. If I listen to the thoughts of others more than I listen to the thoughts of God, it will cause me to have a distorted view of myself and others.

I look back and think about the songs I have connected to the most in my life. And the themes of most of them were about wanting to be loved, rejection, worthlessness, and anger. I believe movies and video games can impact us in the same way as music and written words can. Therefore, it is vital for us to be cautious of what we allow to pass through our ear and eye gates. Ever been heartbroken from love and listened to some sappy song about lost love only to find yourself more brokenhearted or depressed? Ever been angry and listened to anger rock and found yourself even more angry? It is a very sneaky tactic from the enemy to keep us in bondage and living out of our soul. It is such a vicious cycle, one we do not even realize we are in.

The enemy hates us and cannot stand when his plans to destroy us are thwarted. Therefore, he never stops coming at us. This is the reason I have had to make a personal choice to steer clear of most secular music 98 percent of the time. For me, I love worship music. Worship shifts our mindsets; it changes the way we see others and ourselves. It also gives me the opportunity to stay in a place of gratitude instead of being stuck in my feelings.

Day 18 Reflection

While pondering on today's topic, here are some great questions my associate pastor mentioned you can reflect on. He said a great way to check out where your soul is, is by asking yourself questions like "What song am I connecting with the most right now, and why am I connecting to it?" You can also ask yourself, "What is in me that has me connecting to this specific song?"

If you are willing to ask yourself these questions and ask the Lord about them, He will show you the root of why you are connecting with a certain song or type of music. He will also heal you and uproot everything that is not of Him if you will allow Him access to you, even your darkest and most cavernous places. I know it's scary. But, beloved, it is so worth it in the end when you have been transformed into a new person, a person who craves to walk a holy life and step into greater things of the Lord.

I would also encourage you to begin to spend time listening to worship throughout your day. You can listen in your car, while you exercise, or while you are sitting on your porch after work each evening. There will be times I just go outside; I play worship music and sing and dance before the Lord. I promise you it pleases Him greatly and it will transform and bring life to you.

Day 19

They hatch adders' eggs; they weave the spider's
web; he who eats their eggs dies, and from
one that is crushed a viper is hatched.

—Isaiah 59:5 (ESV)

You shall not fear them, for it is the Lord
your God who fights for you.

—Deuteronomy 3:22 (ESV)

Bless those who curse you, pray for
those who are abusive to you.

—Luke 6:28 (NASB)

Life is not without pain and suffering. This pain can crush us where it brings forth a viper inside of us making us say and do things to hurt people because we ourselves are in pain. This viper can make us lash out and corrupt us into becoming hard and vengeful. It can make us feel safe and protected. This viper can become a comfort and a shield from the cold world surrounding us where it makes us feel like it is our only protection.

However, my beloved, it is a lie. It is a deceitful darkness that will coil around us like a python, squeezing the life out of us and destroying everyone around us.

The good news is we do not have to fight for ourselves. It is the Lord our God who fights for us. It is He who defends us, wins the battle, and then calls it our victory. God is such a good Father. He goes before us and behind us and surrounds us with His protection as we walk out what He has called us to do.

Yet, when we try to fight our own battles, especially when we are unhealed, we end up putting ourselves in the position of God where we have become judge and jury toward others. This will cause us to make judgments against people, to lash out at them, and to find ways to hurt them for hurting us.

This is not God's way, and it tells the Father we cannot trust Him to fight on our behalf. There are also consequences for trying to be God, making judgments against others, and lashing out at people, even if it is not intentional. The good news is we can be free from this if we will submit ourselves and our will to the Lord.

Beloved, I am sorry if you have ever felt unprotected from the pains and hurts in life. I am sorry if life has been so painful for you that it brought forth a viper. Unfortunately, we live in a fallen world and were not promised there would be no suffering. Life is unfair at times, and the enemy does not play fair and will take every opportunity to cause destruction in your life. However, the Word of God says there is not one evil thing that has happened to you that God will not use for good (Genesis 50:20).

Today, I would encourage you to ask the Lord to reveal the sources of your pain. The Father is gentle and kind. He will not bring up more than what you can handle. It will probably come out in layers as time passes although He can miraculously heal you in one moment.

I encourage you to repent for trying to stand in God's place by being the judge and jury when you have lashed out at people to protect yourself. By stepping into God's place, what has happened is you have not only judged and tried others but you have also deemed judgment against yourself. You must walk through this to be free, especially if you walk in a victim mentality.

I would seek the Lord to ask His help to forgive those who have hurt you, to ask forgiveness for those you have hurt, and for you to forgive yourself. So often we forget to forgive ourselves, which is just as important as forgiving others.

Ask the Lord to teach you how to trust Him to fight your battles. Bless those who curse you (Romans 12:14), and do not repay evil with evil (1 Peter 3:9). The Father wants you to know He loves you and that you can trust Him. He has your best interest at heart because He designed you and knows everything about you.

<u>Personal Notes</u>

Day 20

Count it all joy, my brothers, when you meet
trials of various kinds, for you know that the
testing of your faith produces steadfastness.

—James 1:2–3 (ESV)

Have you ever felt like you were the punching bag at a gym where MMA fighters train? After you get a serious beating, here comes another one and another one to take a whack at you.

This is what life can often feel like. Sometimes these beatdowns come from the consequences of our own choices or walking in rebellion against God. However, if you are walking in right standing with God, there might be other reasons you are constantly getting knocked down.

One of those reasons is we might be stuck in the same cycle in life. For example, if you have ever had a job where you had great difficulty with your supervisor and you did not have the ability to walk it out in the way God intended, you might find yourself in the same type of environment again and again. Perhaps you get angry a lot and constantly find yourself in situations that make you angry.

God allows us to repeat the same cycle because we did not pass the test the first time. I know it can be exhausting. But if we look at it in a positive way, the Lord is trying to refine and restore us, and He gives us opportunity after opportunity to pass the test so He can keep moving us forward to where He needs us to be to use the skills we have now learned. The cool thing is we never really fail. We just keep going through the same cycle until we pass. However, the goal is to get to a place where we have great revelation and have submitted ourselves to the Lord that it does not take a multitude of times to pass through these cycles and tests. Just know the Lord must test us because He is building fortitude inside us so we will not crumble under the enemy's attacks. He is also using these cycles to build our character.

Another reason we can often feel we keep getting a serious beating is because of our calling. In one of John Paul Jackson's classes I once took, he spoke the higher the mountain of our calling is, the lower our valleys would be. He also mentioned the broader our mountain is, the wider our valleys would be.

So, if you are given the gift of prophecy, you may struggle with your tongue. If you are called to heal the sick, you may struggle with illness. If you are called to heal the brokenhearted, you may struggle with being brokenhearted. I promise there is purpose for this type of pain and training.

Day 20 Reflection

M y friend, you have an adversary that is trying to take you out and prevent you from fulfilling what God has created you to do. It would be easy to let yourself stay down after you keep getting punched. However, there is something inside of you that someone else needs. So I encourage you to stand back up, declare that God's purposes will come to pass in your life, and keep moving ahead. These valleys are great training ground for you for what lies ahead.

If your constant battles are coming from needing to pass a test, poor choices, or walking in disobedience to God, I would encourage you to have a conversation with the Father about it and repent as needed. He will be excited that you have come to Him. He wants nothing more than to help you as His child to become restored and to walk in right standing and alignment with Him. The Lord desires to use you as His holy vessel, and He needs you to accomplish His will on the earth. As His child, He also wants to bless you with many rewards for your obedience, not only in heaven but on earth as well.

Tell Him what is on your mind and heart today and let Him walk you through whatever the situation may be. Let Him comfort you and cover you during this part of your journey. Sometimes we need to ask the Father to hide us during certain seasons in life. As you are walking through this process, I declare a renewed strength over you and that you will run and not grow weary (Isaiah 40:31).

Day 21

And God is able to make all grace abound to you,
so that having all sufficiency in all things at all
times, you may abound in every good work.

—2 Corinthians 9:8 (ESV)

Do not be anxious about anything, but in
everything by prayer and supplication with
thanksgiving, present your requests to God.

—Philippians 4:6 (ESV)

Out of all the beings that God created, we are by far His favorite. We were made in the very image of the Father. We are His children, the sons and daughters of the King of kings, the Almighty God, Ruler of all heaven and earth.

Yet, we often forget who we are. We forget that we are royalty and heirs to a kingdom that is not of this world. We forget as the children of a loving Father, He will provide everything we need to accomplish what He has called us to do. Please believe that whatever God has called you to do, He will give you provision to do it.

However, we seem to get ourselves tangled up because of how we have misinterpreted how the Father works. We do this by telling God how to provide for us and even will try to name our provision. We seem to think we know better than God and ask Him for the things we think we need instead of just asking the Lord for His provision. He already knows exactly what we need to accomplish His will on the earth.

One time, during a conversation with a friend of mine, I realized I had told God how much money I wanted to make, like what my goal income was. After the conversation, I realized that I had declared to the Almighty God what income I thought I should make. I felt it was a humble amount and a reasonable goal; however, what I did not understand was that I put a ceiling over myself and blocked myself from ever going above that amount.

After I repented, a few short months later, for the first time in my life, I had gone over the income amount I set for myself. This was a miracle! I had just started a new job in the same career field but was losing about $350 a month in the switch. Then the Lord blessed me by allowing those lost wages to be recovered. I also earned over the income goal I had set for myself due to some extra funding. See what happens when we just ask God to guide us down the path He has for us and give us provision instead of dictating to Him how to provide for us.

Day 21 Reflection

As you reflect today on provision, I want you to really understand what provision really means according to your calling. Before you were born, God already knew everything about you. He wrote a book about your life and what He has called you. It is the greatest story waiting to be revealed through relationship and intimacy with the Father, one that requires a willing heart and radical obedience. What God wrote about your life is greater than anything you could have ever imagined for yourself. As you walk out your calling, the Father already knows what you need to fulfill your purpose. He will always give you everything you need to accomplish His will.

Provision is not just about financial means; it is also about placing people you will need in your life along the way through divine appointments and friendships to help you. It is about giving you the gifts and anointing you need to achieve the assignment He has given you.

Now that you understand one of the ways God provides is based on your calling, there are other types of provision and things that God does to provide for you or your family. Maybe it is material items, healing, food, and salvation for friends and family.

As you lift your needs for provision to the Lord, the one thing I pray you take away from today is that we do not tell

God how to provide for us. We do not tell God how to save our lost loved one. We do not tell Him we need to win the lottery to do His will. We do not tell God how we want Him to heal us.

As the children of a good Father, all we must do is simply go to Him with thanksgiving, tell Him of our needs, and come into agreement with how He wants to accomplish providing for us. If you have dictated to the Lord how you want Him to provide for you, I would ask that you prayerfully repent because it could be blocking the Lord's ability to work in your life. It can also be blocking your blessings.

We must understand we are not God and we often do not realize that we so easily step into His role, which shoves Him to the side. Therefore, we end up using the Father for what we want or need, which shows Him that we do not trust Him to bring provision, that we are selfish, and that we do not love Him just because He is our Father.

Beloved, if that is the type of relationship you have had with the Lord, it is not too late to ask for forgiveness and move into the most beautiful relationship you will ever have. Your cup will run over if you choose the better thing. I guarantee it.

Day 22

I praise you, for I am fearfully and wonderfully
made. Wonderful are your works; my soul
knows it very well. My frame was not hidden
from you, when I was being made in secret,
intricately woven in the depths of the earth.
Your eyes saw my unformed substance; in your
book were written, every one of them, the days
that were formed for me, when as yet there was
none of them. How precious to me are your
thoughts, O God! How vast is the sum of them!

—Psalm 139:14–17 (ESV)

While our natural mother and father brought us into the world, they are merely stewards of us. God is our true Father. While we may look like our natural mother and father and carry their genes, we are truly made in the image of God. He created us and knew us before we were ever born. He is delighted in us, rejoices with gladness over us, and sings over us (Zephaniah 3:17). He has kept track of our sorrow and tears and has collected those tears in a bottle (Psalm 56:8).

I do not know what your life has been like. Some of you may have had a great childhood with amazing and loving parents. You may only have a few wounds that have carried with you through life. It is okay. This can still apply to you because even those tiny hurts can impact everything we do in life. It can affect how we feel about ourselves, how we treat people, our ability to trust, and even the choices we make. Others have gone through severe pain and suffering growing up and have been left with deep wounds.

Did you know that the way you feel about your natural parents reflects on how you feel about God as Father, Jesus, and Holy Spirit? The Father represents your natural father. The Holy Spirit represents your natural mother. And, Jesus, He represents your friends, siblings, and extended family like cousins.

How you relate to each of the Trinity (Father, Son, and Holy Spirit) is typically based on how you feel about your family in the natural world. This means that if you have or had a harsh and uncaring father in the natural world, you may have the mindset that God as Father is harsh and cruel. If you have or had a difficult relationship with your mother, it can affect your ability to hear the Holy Spirit and interact with Him. If there was discord between you and your siblings or maybe you were an only child, you might struggle seeing Jesus as your friend.

If you were missing a father, mother, or close family throughout your life, especially in your childhood, perhaps you are not sure how to relate to any of the Trinity. It is not too late for you to run into the arms of the Father so He can show you the depths of His love and restore you.

Day 22 Reflection

F riend, I have cried many tears from childhood trauma. The Lord has healed me of many wounds and continues to heal me to this day. I want the same for you. So my husband, John, and I would like to stand together in place of your mother, father, and siblings (identification repentance). And we would like to repent on behalf of the hurt they may have caused you.

Beloved, we are sorry for the hurt we have caused you, whether it was intentional or unintentional. You are the Father's greatest treasure, and we repent for not stewarding the responsibility He gave us to care for you as He intended. We repent for not treating you like you were beloved and for misrepresenting God to you. We apologize that you could not see and feel how much God loves you through our actions toward you.

We repent for every word or action done in anger or frustration, every time we made you feel worthless or unloved. We repent for any abusive act (physical, sexual, emotional) we took against you. We repent for treating you as if you should be seen and not heard or telling you your voice did not matter. We repent for every time we ignored or neglected you. We repent for every time we made promises we did not keep and for not cherishing the time we had with you.

We repent for everything we have said or done that made you feel unapproved of or that you were not good enough. We repent for the times we have not protected you from harm and were not your shelter in the storm. We repent for not setting boundaries for you and training you up in the way you should go. We repent for any word curses we have spoken against you.

We ask the Lord to sever any unhealthy soul ties between us. We pray lies will be shattered and agreements with those lies will be burned up. We ask You to begin the healing process now, Lord Jesus, in our beloved child. We ask You to help them to forgive us so they can be released from carrying unforgiveness that will eventually destroy them.

Holy Spirit, we ask that Your presence be known and that our precious child will feel the Father's embrace and love. We thank You for them and that they were born. They are not a mistake, accident, or burden. They are truly a blessing and a miracle. We ask You to restore them so they can walk out what You wrote over their life. In the name Jesus. Amen.

<u>Personal Notes</u>

Day 23

And the Lord will make you the head and not the tail,
and you will only be above and not underneath, if you
listen to the commandments of the Lord your God which
I am commanding you today, to follow them carefully.

—Deuteronomy 28:13 (NASB)

You are the light of the world. A city
on a hill cannot be hidden.

—Matthew 5:14 (ESV)

But you are a chosen people, a royal priesthood, a holy
nation, a people for his own possession. As a result,
you can show others the goodness of God, for he called
you out of the darkness into his wonderful light.

—1 Peter 2:9 (ESV)

At every turn in the Bible, the Word of God communicates who we are to the Father, what His thoughts are about us, and how much He loves us. He also tries to show us what our identity is in Him. Our identity must come from Him and only Him and not in what we accomplish and what we do for a living or from any titles we have. So much of our time is spent on trying to be somebody we do not realize we already are somebody, a very special someone in the eyes of our Father.

We do not have to perform to win the Father's heart or His love; we already have it. We do not need to pursue perfection because the only perfection that ever existed is Jesus. If you have not learned this by now, chasing perfection, something that does not exist, is very exhausting. It wears us down.

This pursuit makes us feel we have failed if we do not meet the unrealistic expectations we have set for ourselves or the ones others have set for us. This causes us to become fractured and gives the enemy access to oppress us with his lies of failure, disappointment in ourselves, and unworthiness. It can also cause us serious health issues from stress, fear, and anxiety.

Let these verses be written on your heart so you know who you are and who you belong to so you can rest in His peace as you go about each day.

Today, my husband, John, and I would like to honor you by giving you a mother and father blessing. Having a parental blessing is very important, and you can read throughout the Bible blessings were given to children.

Beloved, we are so thankful you were born. We thank God you were born for such a time as this (Esther 4:14) to partner with the Father to destroy the assignment of the enemy and to bring heaven to earth.

We want you to know you are the head and not the tail. You are above and not beneath. You are blessed when you are coming and going. We pray the Lord will go before you to prepare the way, guide your path, and be your rearguard to protect you.

We declare restoration and wholeness over your life and that you will walk in complete victory. We speak crop failure over the enemy's assignment over your life. We pray that you will not buckle to fear, doubt, or anxiety and your identity will be completely found in the Lord. We pray you will walk through every trial with joy and know the Father has already won the battle for you and you have already overcome. We pray the Father will hide you from your enemies and no weapon formed against you shall prosper (Isaiah 54:17). We declare that every arrow the enemy shoots to attack you will return to the enemy's camp, leaving you untouched.

We pray you will have revelation of what God has written about you so you can accomplish His will for your life. We pray for timely provision in every assignment given by the Lord. We pray you will come into agreement and be radically obedient to what the Father has called you to do and you will do it with a willing heart. We declare, as you follow the leading of the Lord, that you will be overflowing with fruitfulness and there will be no barrenness inside of you.

We pray you will have a desire to know and encounter the deeper things of God and you will run after Him and all that He has to offer. We pray you will seek out and ask Him for the gifts of the Holy Spirit (1 Corinthians 12:8–10). We pray you will walk in brokenness before the Lord and humility. We pray you will walk in honor and integrity and pursue living a holy life in relationship with the Lord instead of walking in religion. We pray you will forgive so you can be forgiven. We pray you will allow the Lord to fight your battle so you can be found blameless in His sight. We pray you will walk in His peace, even in the midst of life's storms. We declare that when you are weary, you will have your strength renewed so you can soar. We pray that you will become love, finish the race set before you, and know that the Father is pleased with you.

You are precious and loved so much, and we pray you never forget you are a great treasure to us. We pray this in the name of Jesus. Amen.

Day 24

Do not judge, so you will not be judged.

—Matthew 7:1 (NASB)

Do not judge by the outward appearance,
but judge with righteous judgment.

—John 7:24 (NASB)

One of the greatest lessons I have learned in life is about judgment. What I have learned about judgment came from a book my apostle recommended called *How to Stop the Pain* by Dr. James B. Richards. I once heard Apostle Tim say when he started handing these books out, it cut down his counseling sessions by 50 percent. This book is that good and is still currently on my top five list of favorite books I have ever read.

When we look at a deed or an action, we can look at it and judge whether it is sin or not because we know and understand the Word of God. As our intimate relationship with the Father grows, we can judge whether something is good or godly because while there are things that might be permissible, not everything is beneficial (1 Corinthians 10:23). These are the things I believe are righteous judgment.

However, there is a different judgment I would like to focus on today.

We can observe and recognize what someone has said or done, but this is not judgment. It is merely what we have observed or have experienced. Judgment comes in when we choose to make a determination regarding why the person behaved in a certain manner. This determination is based on total assumption because in truth, we often have no idea why a person did what they did. It is our assumption of why a person did what they did that takes us into a place of judgment.

For example, if I ask my husband to pick up something for me before I get home from work and, when I get home, I see the item is not there, this is merely something I have observed. If I start to speculate why it is not there, this is the moment I could step into judgment. Maybe I assume he does not care about me or he is insensitive to my needs. If I go there, I have just made a judgment about him. In all honesty, it could have been the item was out of stock or perhaps he got sick and needed to stay home that day. However, I have already made a judgment against him because I made an assumption about what he did not do.

Maybe someone has treated us in a certain way, and we do not know why. It is so easy to allow our mind to start spinning with theories on why they did what they did. We must not go there because once we begin judging others, we leave ourselves wide open to be judged by others.

Day 24 Reflection

In most of us, making a judgment about why someone did what they did has become second nature. For many of us, making a judgment is unintentional, and we do not even realize what we are doing. However, we are still accountable for our behavior, and there are still consequences in the natural world and in the spirit that we will have to face if we continue making judgments against others.

Judgment will become a huge tree with a tremendous root system in your life if you have spent years making judgments against others. It is the cause of much of the pain in our own lives. The good news is this tree of judgment can be uprooted and we can walk in freedom from judging others and being judged by others.

Today, as you reflect, ask the Holy Spirit to reveal to you the judgments you have made against others or even yourself. It is important to repent for any judgments He brings to your mind. Ask the Lord to forgive you from any lies that you have believed about someone or yourself. Then ask Him to release you and the other person involved from the consequences of the judgments you have made.

Also, it is a good idea to ask the Lord if you need to make amends with the individual you judged. Sometimes restitution is a part of the process to right a wrong. Follow the Holy Spirit as He leads.

I will tell you, since making judgments is such a part of our lives in society, it is a hard habit to break without divine intervention. However, as you repent, the Lord can break it off you piece by piece as you pursue His heart for people. Ask the Father to help you see people through His eyes and to love them as He loves them.

Day 25

And let us not grow weary of doing good, for in
due season we will reap, if we do not give up.

—Galatians 6:9 (ESV)

Yet those who wait for the Lord Will gain new strength;
They will mount up with wings like eagles, They will run
and not get tired, They will walk and not become weary.

—Isaiah 40:31 (NASB)

Life is full of seasons, some where we are walking in the
mountains, which is wonderful. Then there are the seasons where we travel through the valley, which, quite frankly,
is not typically fun or easy. During the seasons we are in the
valley, we often become exhausted, we lose our peace, we end
up crawling, and we want to give up. It happens to most if
not all of us at some point in our lives.

The valley seasons, like the wilderness seasons, are very
important in our lives. These seasons stretch us, they test our
character, they refine us, and they train us for upcoming seasons. In the valley, we find out what we are truly made of and
whether we are walking in our own strength or leaning on
the Lord to be our strength.

Beloved, no matter what kind of season we are walking in or how difficult it may be, we can walk in joy and peace and not be weary.

<h1 style="text-align:center">Day 25 Revelation</h1>

As you reflect, do you know what type of season you are in? Are you in a mountain season where everything is going well? If so, are you honoring the Lord with thanksgiving for being in such a good season? Are you in a season where you are walking in the valley? If so, are you praising God for what He is doing in your life even though it may feel rough?

If you do not experience seasons of walking in the valley, you may need to have a conversation with the Lord to find out if you are walking down the path He created for you. If you are walking down the path He created for you, you are a threat to the enemy. This means you should be walking in the valley at times and facing some opposition.

Today, I would like to pray for you so you can find joy in all things, even in the seasons where you are walking in a valley.

Beloved, I pray for you as you walk through difficult seasons. I pray you will submit yourselves to them willingly so the Lord can begin a good work inside of you. I pray you will have radical obedience to do as the Lord requires during these seasons, so they are not lengthened due to your resistance.

I pray in the valley you will be refined so you can become more like Jesus. I pray you will not look at these seasons as punishment but as a beautification and strengthening process. I pray you choose not to grumble and complain (Philippians 2:14), but you find joy in all circumstances (James 1:2). I pray the Father will surround you with His peace and that you will not only walk in peace but your presence will also usher in peace for others in the midst of their life's storms.

I pray you will not become weary or give up because, my friend, there is a broad opening waiting for you around the corner of the narrow path you are walking through. I pray the Lord will renew your strength so you can keep pressing on and moving forward. You can do this because you can do all things through Christ Jesus (Philippians 4:13). I ask this in the name of Jesus. Amen.

Day 26

Beloved, do not be surprised at the fiery trial
when it comes upon you to test you, as though
something strange were happening to you.

—1 Peter 4:12 (ESV)

These things I have spoken to you so that in Me you
may have peace. In the world you will have tribulation;
but take courage; I have overcome the world.

—John 16:33 (NASB)

In Isaiah 54:17, the Bible says that no weapon formed against us will prosper, but this does not mean weapons will not be formed. In fact, if we are a true follower of Jesus, the enemy has placed a target on our back. His sole purpose is to bring death and destruction to our lives, and he will try to attack us at every turn to keep us from fulfilling God's purposes for our lives. If we are not constantly under fire from the enemy, we may have to reevaluate our relationship with the Lord.

We were created to make our enemy, Satan, tremble. We were created to destroy his works as we partner with the Lord to bring heaven to earth. This is serious business not to be taken lightly. Please understand you are going to face trials and tribulations in life. However, how we walk through them is entirely up to us. We do not have to buckle to fear because God did not give us a spirit of fear (2 Timothy 1:7). We can walk in complete confidence knowing the battle has been won.

Please do not misunderstand me. Fear is natural; fear helps us survive. Fear brings forth the fight-or-flight instincts God put inside of us, which activate to help us avoid danger. However, when we allow fear to overcome us, we can become susceptible to a spirit of fear. This spirit can wreak all kinds of destruction in our lives, and it simply sneaks in when we walk in fear and do not ask for God to intervene to overcome. This spirit of fear paralyzes us. And the next thing we know, we are not only afraid of what initially made us fearful but we are now fearful of men, illness, and our future, to leave our home, or of anything in life. Everything that manifests in our lives starts from a simple seed that is planted, whether bad or good.

The good news is Jesus already has overcome the world. He has overcome your trial. He has overcome your battles and won them for you and then calls them your victory. He has given us the ability to trample on snakes and scorpions (Luke 10:19) and walk in peace. So be encouraged! We already have victory.

Today, as you reflect, I would like to give you some things to consider and ask the Lord about.

First, if you are not under constant attack from the enemy and you seem to have a peaceful existence, are you even a threat to him and his kingdom of darkness? Second, if you are under attack, is it because of your personal choices that allow the enemy to have legal access to you? If not and it is just because you are chasing after the things of God, know that God is with you.

I know these are tough questions to have to ask yourself, but I have had to ask myself these same questions. It is not an easy process because it often exposes things inside of us that are not of the Lord or things we do not like about ourselves. My hope is that you do not take offense, but you understand my prayer is that through revelation you will have restoration in your life.

Another thing I would encourage you to reflect on is fear. Do you find yourself constantly afraid? Do you shudder at the news when all they seem to focus on is natural disasters, bloodshed, and illness? If so, perhaps it is time to turn the television off for a season, set yourself apart with the Lord, and focus on listening to what He wants to say about the city, state, or country you reside in. No matter what is going on where you live, God has a redemptive plan for the territory you live in, and He wants to communicate to you what the plan is so you can partner with Him in prayer or action for it to come into fruition.

This is also an opportunity to ask the Father what the root is to your fear, where the fear began. He wants to restore you and will show you exactly the point in your life that fear became rooted inside of you. Once you know what that root is, you can repent or forgive as necessary. Then ask the Lord to uproot whatever it is so you can walk in faith and assurance that no matter what is going on in the world, you can walk in His peace knowing He has already overcome on your behalf.

Day 27

Now he called the twelve together and
gave them power and authority over all the
demons, and the power to heal diseases.

—Luke 9:1 (NASB)

Behold, I give you authority to tread on snakes
and scorpions, and over all the power of the
enemy, and nothing shall hurt you.

—Luke 10:19 (ESV)

As you read the Bible, you will find many references to the power and authority God has given us here on earth. This power and authority have been given to all, not just some, not just someone who carries the title of pastor or priest. Sometimes it can be confusing to understand what it means to have power and authority. It may lead you to wonder, *What is the difference between power and authority?*

The word *power* is used to describe the ability to do something. It can be physical ability to lift weights or to run. It can be the ability to heal or to create something. While power is the ability to do a certain thing, authority is the permission from heaven to wield and execute power over a certain thing or situation.

One of the things I hope you take away from today is the fact that you may have the ability to do something; however, it does not mean you have the authority to do it. Again, authority comes from heaven where God has given you permission to wield power. Authority is given to us for many reasons. It can be where we need specific authority to accomplish God's purpose over our lives, or it can be something we have earned because we have overcome in a specific area. For example, if I have overcome anger, then I now carry authority over anger and can help someone else become free from anger. Others may carry authority over death, addictions, or depression.

There is also authority that God has given to all of us. We all have the power and authority to heal diseases and cast out demons. This was not just for the disciples who walked with Jesus when He was alive. This type of power and authority is for every disciple or follower of Jesus, and this includes you and me. If that does not set a fire in your heart, I am not sure what will.

The other thing I hope you take away from today is that it is so important for your own sake to always ask and listen to what the Lord wants you to do and how He wants you to proceed when it comes to using power and authority. The Holy Spirit must be our guide as a matter of safety and protection for ourselves and everyone else. Being guided prevents us from stepping into our soul, which can cause us to misuse what God has given us and allow the enemy access to us.

I get really excited about using power and authority, because it brings healing, restoration, and God's plans into fruition and destroys the works of the enemy.

If you have ever seen any of the *Spider-Man* movies, there is a line "With great power comes great responsibility." This is exactly how I believe we should use our authority to wield power. It must come from a place of brokenness before the Lord, fear of the Lord, and humility.

Have you ever considered the power and authority that have been given to you? Have you thought about having a conversation with the Lord about any specific authority He has given you? Is there some area God has brought you restoration that you now have authority over? If you do use your authority, do you use it to act on the behalf of what God has spoken to you?

What an interesting conversation to have with the Lord today. As you reflect, I would encourage you to consider asking the Father to give you a desire for a deeper relationship with Him. As you are growing in Him, ask for an understanding of power and authority. Ask Him to train you to use the authority and power He has given you with wisdom and humility. If you still are not sure about these things and whether or not they are real for today, ask the Lord for revelation. If you earnestly seek Him and the things of Him, His Word says He will show you (Jeremiah 29:13).

Lastly, make sure your first love is always the Father and not the gifts and anointings. You want to be loved for who you are and not what you can give someone. God is the same way. It grieves Jesus when we just call on Him for what He can give us. He greatly desires our attention, affection, and wants to be ministered to. He is our greatest love and our greatest treasure because He gave all for us. Everything else is just an amazing and wild bonus.

Day 28

You will also decide and decree a thing, and it
will be established for you; And the light [of
God's favor] will shine upon your ways.

—Job 22:28 (AMP)

So shall my word be that goes out of my mouth; it shall
not return to me empty, but it shall accomplish that which
I purpose, and shall succeed in the thing for which I sent.

—Isaiah 55:11 (ESV)

Every person who is a follower of Jesus is given the opportunity to speak on God's behalf. To take on that role, one must know God intimately, know His ways, understand His heart for all His creation, listen when He speaks, and willingly obey.

When we have an intimate relationship with the Father, He will reveal to us hidden things (Jeremiah 33:3). He can reveal to us aspects about a person's life. He can reveal information regarding our city or country, political leaders, and upcoming trials the body of Christ will face.

As the Lord reveals things to us, He will often give us the authority to decree aloud what He spoke to us. A decree is an official order issued by a legal authority. This means the God of the entire universe has given us permission to speak out what He has spoken to us. Friends, decreeing something is not speaking out our opinions, thoughts, wishes, or desires. When we decree, we are only speaking aloud what God tells us to say, nothing more, nothing less. When we decree aloud, it releases something into the atmosphere that starts to move things in the natural world and in the spirit realm. Can you believe it? Can you believe the Lord of heaven and earth wants to use average people like you and me to move mountains, to shift the atmosphere, and to destroy the works of the enemy? I mean, let me be honest, He could do anything He wants on His own. However, He desires greatly to partner with those who are willing to be used as His pure and holy vessels.

The enemy has sold us all a lie to think we are worthless, have no value, and lack purpose. And it has not taken him much effort to have deceived us. The Father needs us to awaken from our sleep, rise, and learn to hear what He is saying to us so we can decree it. If we do not, the world will continue to fall into darkness. We can no longer afford to be the church that has been lulled to sleep and indoctrinated to think God will take care of everything and we just need to stand by and wait for Him to move. Yes, God is in control, but He put us here on the earth to take dominion over it (Genesis 1:26–28), not to sit back on the couch praying and hoping He will deliver us as we sit and wait for the rapture. Part of our kingdom inheritance requires responsibility; it requires action to stand up and decree God's Word so the kingdom of darkness will be pushed back. I encourage you to take part in all the Father has to offer. He needs us.

<h1 style="text-align:center">Day 28 Reflection</h1>

I feel like with each day, we have gone deeper into the things of the Lord. I would lie to you if I were to say I was not completely fascinated by and in awe with the amazing God we serve. He has been so good to me, and I could shout from the mountaintops of what He has done for me. He has taken me from walking in severe depravity and darkness and transformed me into someone who carries His light and His love.

If you do not have a deep and intimate relationship with the Lord, I would encourage you to seek Him because He is chasing after you with all His might. He wants you to walk in everything He has for you and everything He wrote about you before you were ever born. As you do this, He will begin revealing many things to you.

If you feel you struggle hearing the Lord clearly, repent for any known and unknown sins you have. Repent for any times you have declared that you could not hear the Lord or any times you heard the Lord but chose to disobey. Ask Him to remove anything that is blocking you from being able to hear Him clearly. Then position yourself to be able to hear Him. This might mean you need to put your phone on silent, turn off the radio and television, and get to a place where you feel God's presence the most.

When you find that place, practice being still and silent, which is not so easy considering the fast-paced and busy lives most of us lead. Maybe you love being out in nature and walking in the woods. Being in nature is where I often feel closest to the Lord. Find your place and just be with the Lord.

When you have positioned yourself to hear the Lord, start with fifteen minutes at a time and just sit in silence without any distractions. When you read your Bible, ask the Lord what He wants to reveal to you in what you just read. A relationship is two-sided; it is intimate friendship and even a love affair. It takes practice and work. You will get there with time. As you learn to hear the Father clearly, He can show you what is hidden, and you will know what to decree as you are praying. Then rest in knowing you were obedient and see how He begins to move on your behalf. He needs you, mighty warrior! He needs you trained and ready for battle.

Day 29

A joyful heart is good medicine, but a
crushed spirit dries up the bones.

—Proverbs 17:22 (ESV)

Is anyone among you sick? Let him call for the
elders of the church, and let them pray over him,
anointing him with oil in the name of the Lord.

—James 5:14 (ESV)

Healing is a very controversial topic, but I feel I am called to speak about it, in a loving manner.

There are many people who believe that healing and miracles are not for today, but I would encourage those people to get into their Bible and do the research. It is not difficult to find verses about healing and disease in the Old and New Testaments.

I have been curious about healing for a very long time. For years I struggled with chronic pain and illness, which made me determined to find answers. Since then, I have been healed miraculously of some things that I suffered with, both physically and emotionally. Most of my healing has come from walking through repentance, inner healing, and deliverance.

What I have come to understand is over 80 percent of diseases and illnesses have a spiritual root. The other percentage is from mere accidents that occur. When I speak about spiritual roots, I am speaking about there being a spiritual root that causes mental and physical disease and illness. In the book *Exposing the Spiritual Roots to Disease* by Dr. Henry Wright, Dr. Wright talks about how spiritually rooted diseases come from separation, separation from God, ourselves, or others. This means somewhere there is a breach in our relationships, whether it is our relationship with the Father; our friends, family, or coworkers; or even ourselves.

Some of these spiritual roots are bitterness, unforgiveness, self-hate, shame, guilt, anger, and fear. Whether we realize it or not, the things I just mentioned are a form of sin, and the Bible explains that the wage of sin is death (Romans 6:23). As we carry these things inside of us, they eat away at our bodies or minds and cause disease and illness.

We were meant to go into eternity at full strength. We were never meant to die an early death, and we do not have to allow our health to be stolen from us. The journey back to good health and overcoming disease and illness is all about reconciliation. It is about getting back into right relationship with the Father and walking through a restorative process with ourselves and others. This reconciliation repairs the breach of separation and allows our health to become restored.

Day 29 Reflection

B eloved, I know it is difficult to ponder on such tough topics. It is often hard to look deep inside of ourselves because we are afraid of what we might see or afraid we will not like what we will find. So we ignore self-reflection and try to hide the dark and cavernous places from the Lord. However, the Father already knows, and He is just waiting for us to open ourselves up to Him.

If we are willing to put in the work and find out what the spiritual root causes are for the diseases and illnesses we have, we can walk through repentance and inner healing, which can lead to physical healing. I wish I had the time to tell you about all the ways God has healed me as I have walked through repentance and inner healing.

One of the best resources I have found is a book by Dr. Henry Wright titled *A More Excellent Way*. This book is a serious guide to helping one find the spiritual root of pretty much every disease. It has been a great tool to help me in my journey to become fully restored and walk in complete wholeness.

To walk through the process of restoration, you must begin by repairing the breach in your relationship with the Lord. Ask the Father to show you where there might be any areas you need to be reconciled with Him. As you do that, you can also ask Him about the breaches that need to be dealt with in your relationships or with yourself.

A breach with the Lord might look like living in disobedience regarding something the Lord has asked you to do, or it could be that you do not trust Him. A breach with someone you know might be where you have unforgiveness or bitterness toward them. A breach with yourself might look like you holding on to self-hate, shame, or condemnation. Whatever you are holding on to, it is making your body and mind sick, giving you migraines, lowering your immune system, and causing dementia, high blood pressure, cancer, and so much more.

As you begin to walk in reconciliation, just spend time with the Lord asking Him if there are things you are holding onto that you need to release. He will lead the way. There are other things that can block you from healing besides separation in relationships. Walking in willful sin or unbelief that an individual can be healed can block healing as well. So, if those are things you are struggling with, I would encourage you to lay your cards out on the table and ask the Lord to help you with your unbelief and turn your heart so you will hate sin. God is a good Father, and He wants and needs you to be restored. Love, it is not part of His plan for you to be tormented, sick, and weary. Every step you take, every act of repentance, and everything you are willing to lay before the feet of Jesus is worth it all to walk in right relationship with the Father and to be made whole in your spirit, body, mind, and soul.

Day 30

I know this has been quite the journey for you, and I have no doubt if you are sincerely pursuing the Father, you are on the right track to walk in complete restoration. As we finish out our thirty days, I wanted to leave you with some extra important pieces of revelation as you continue to walk through healing and deliverance. It will help you grow and mature in the ways of the Lord.

- As you are walking through healing and restoration, you will be tested, and you may fall. It is pretty much guaranteed and comes with the territory of being an imperfect human. However, as you fall, keep a "yes" in your spirit and get back up. The Lord can do a lot for you if you will keep saying yes to the things of the Lord. Also, the Holy Spirit is sent to convict us of our sins, which makes us want to turn back to God. We must never allow ourselves to walk in shame or condemnation because it is not from the Lord; it is another tactic of the enemy to keep us in bondage.

- Ask for the Lord's grace to help you when you fall. Grace is not there as a fail-safe for us to use so casually. Many people have the mindset that "If I cannot control myself and fall into sin or if I just do this one more time, God's grace will cover me." We cannot abuse God's grace by sinning and then asking for God's grace. The Lord's grace is Him empowering us and strengthening us to where we do not sin. Yet, if we unintentionally sin, His grace does cover us. However, some people use God's grace as a "get out of jail free" card because they do not really understand what grace really is.

- Worship and praise is vital to healing, restoration, and growing in the Lord, especially during difficult seasons. Worship is offering thanksgiving to the Father, and it honors Him. Worship is also a type of warring. When we are in a place of true surrender and we worship, we cannot be depressed or ungrateful. So it helps us walk in the opposite spirit of what the enemy wants to do in our lives. It is powerful, pleases the Lord greatly, and allows His spirit to flow and move.

- If you are not filled with the Holy Spirit and do not pray in the spirit, I would encourage you to grab ahold of that opportunity as fast as you can. Sometimes it is hard to pray in the natural because we do not always know what to pray. Praying in the spirit bypasses your soul, moves you out of the way, and allows the Holy Spirit to pray on your behalf straight to the Father. You may not know what you are praying, but the Lord does, and it is good.

- As you walk through the journey of just being in relationship with the Father and you are growing, falling, growing, being tested, falling, and so on, do not be hard on yourself. The Father delights in you, and He is there every step of the way. Just get back up, press on, and remember where you used to be and where you are. Be thankful you are not who you used to be and give glory to God for all the good work He has done inside of you. Rome was not built in a day, and neither is anything that God wants to do in your life. Take a deep breath, exhale, offer yourself some grace, and have some fun along the way.

Day 30 Reflection

Today, I think it is important to just sit back and reflect on how much the Father loves you and how much He has done in your life over these last thirty days or however long you have spent going through this book. Do you feel you have a better understanding of certain things you have been questioning? Do you feel lighter? Do you feel anything has shifted inside of you? Assess yourself in your body, mind, behavior, or personality to see if you notice any changes.

I honor you for walking through this journey. It is not an easy one. It is one I have walked through myself and one I continue to walk through daily. Healing and deliverance is something we will have to walk through for the rest of our lives. However, it is truly a blessing from the Lord.

I pray this book has given you revelation and brought you healing in every area of your life. I hope it has given you an understanding of who God has made you to be and has helped you learn you are important to the Father and to the kingdom. You are more than a conqueror, and what you carry inside of you, someone else desperately needs. Therefore, it is important to become mature believers who are walking in restoration. You cannot pour out of an empty or broken cup.

I pray you continue to let the Lord guide you and you will keep growing in your maturity as a believer. I pray you are becoming a mighty man or woman of God and that you will be dangerous for the kingdom. Be blessed, beloved. I am proud of you for taking this journey with me, and I know the Father is proud of you as well.

Personal Notes

Index

Topics listed by days:

About the Author

From the age of seven, Deana Elliott dreamed of being an author and traveling the world. As a child she spent a lot of her time writing poetry and short stories and looking through the pages of her thesaurus. Over the years, the Lord has walked her through extensive restoration from trauma and brokenness. Deana's experience has given her a sincere passion for healing, deliverance, and seeing people walk in complete wholeness. Her heart is to share what she has learned with others so they can know who they are in Christ, feel His love for them, and become who they are created to be.

Deana resides in Bossier City, Louisiana, with her husband, John, and their adorable dog. She is the proud mother of a son who is a veteran of the United States Air Force. An educator by day, Deana received an undergraduate degree in social sciences and a Master of Arts degree in guidance and counseling from Louisiana Tech University. Most of her career has been spent in the field of social services and education.

In her spare time, Deana loves to cook and travel with her husband. She enjoys taking naps, watching Korean drama, having boba tea with friends, going on new adventures, and reading.